My First Acrostic

Sussex & Surrey

Edited by Jenni Bannister

First published in Great Britain in 2011 by:

Young Writers
Remus House
Coltsfoot Drive
Peterborough
PE2 9BF
Telephone: 01733 890066
Website: www.youngwriters.co.uk

All Rights Reserved
© Copyright Contributors 2011
SB ISBN 978-0-85739-455-2

Foreword

The 'My First Acrostic' collection was developed by Young Writers specifically for Key Stage 1 children. The poetic form is simple, fun and gives the young poet a guideline to shape their ideas, yet at the same time leaves room for their imagination and creativity to begin to blossom.

Due to the young age of the entrants we have enjoyed rewarding their effort by including as many of the poems as possible. Our hope is that seeing their work in print will encourage the children to continue writing as they grow and develop their skills into our poets of tomorrow.

Young Writers was established in 1990 to nurture creativity in our children and young adults, to give them an interest in poetry and an outlet to express themselves. This latest collection will act as a milestone for the young poets and one that will be enjoyable to revisit again and again.

To granny and papa

Love
oli
xxx

Contents

Birchwood Grove Community Primary School, Burgess Hill

Jemima Goldsmith (5) 1
Thomas Penswick (5) 1
Rebekah Sayle (6) 2
Daisy Thring (6) 2
Megan Leaney (6) 3
Molly Harrild (6) 3
Dylan Boylett (6) 3
Lily Begum (5) 4
Joshua Kerr (6) 4
Tabitha Hide Stewart (5) 4
Max Spooner (5) 5
Oliver Hester (6) 5
Reuben Kerr (5) 5
Jayden Zhang (6) 6
Daisy Miller (5) 6
Katie O'Toole (5) 7
Maddy Stewart-Parsons (5) 7
Eleanor Cole (6) 8
Katie Hobbs (6) 8
Ethan Hall (6) 9
Holly Izzard (5) 9
Hannah Johanson (5) 10
Jamie Padgham (6) 10
Tallia Clarke (6) 11
Amelie Palmer-Brown (6) 11
Nathan Drake (5) 12
Ryan Goss (5) 12
Mila Anscombe (6) 13
Nathan Ward (5) 13
Isobel Cooper (7) 14
Joel Cragg (5) & Jack Smart (6) 14
Thomas Johnson & Louis White (5) 15
Ruby Mayes (7) 15
Ryan Sargent (7) 16
Georgia McLean (6) 16
Benjamin Pryse (7) 17
Amy Kenward (7) 17
Hannah Jellett (7) 18
Alex Pilbeam (7) 18
Tristan Hepburn (7) 19
Harry Heath (6) 19
Jake Trist (7) 20
Mark Jellett (7) 20
Harry Argles & Toby Lewis (7) 21
Samuel Biss (6) 21
Max Blanthorn (6) 22
James Rose (7) 22
Lucy McNiven (6) 23
Emma Wickens (6) 23
Stephanie Zhou (6) 24
Michael Lea (6) 24

Bosham Primary School, Bosham

George Goldsmith (7) 25
India Rose (7) 25
Mollie Clark (6) 25
Charly Turpin (6) 26
Olivia Toms (7) 26
Tayla Heron (6) 27

Danesfield Manor School, Walton-on-Thames

Joshua Maisuria-Hull (5) 27
Saskia Lawrence (6) 28
Isabella Smith (5) 28
Louis MacDonald (6) 28
Kaya Kondel (5) 29
Annabel Pilgrim (4) 29
Zachary Smith (4) 30
Emily Hewens (4) 30
Samuel Clough (5) 30
Thomas White (5) 31
Laetitia Clift (4) 31
Himmat Bains (4) 32
Bailey MacDonald (4) 32
Theo Marshall (4) 32
Robert Russell (4) 33
Ria Kishani Jayawardene (7) 33
Ahan Sinha (5) 33
Nicole Farmer (6) 34
Madeleine White (6) 34
Helena O'Neill (7) 35
Max Culpin (7) 35

Samuel Wells (6) 36	Keira Clisby (6) 64
Anika Pintos-Cummings (6) 37	Hannah Borthwick (6) 64
Jacques Behier (6) 37	Lucy Herbert (5) 65
Isabella Coro (7) 38	Lauren Kaye (6) 65
Benjamin David Fish (6) 38	Jessica Allen (5) 66
Jamie McNeill (6) 39	Connie Carr (5) 66
Alexandre Lucas (7) 39	Aimee Gould (6) 67
Emilia Cavanagh (6) 40	Ellie Moore (5) 67
	Stefan Avramov (6) 68

Hall Grove School, Bagshot

Claudia Platts (6) 40	Éloise Bastille (7) 69
Max Tenenbaum (7) 41	Harriet Price (5) 70
Millie Padfield (6) 41	Jack Blamire (5) 71
Charlie Wyatt (6) 42	Jamie Sice (7) 72
Elea Tulloch (7) 42	Lottie Jackson (6) 72
Owen Young (6) 43	Caspar Watson-Hart (5) 73
Billy Easeman (6) 43	Lauren Hawes (6) 74
Emily Myers (7) 44	Charlie Rose (6) 75
Manu Prasad (7) 44	Harvey Harriss (5) 76
Archie Graham (6) 45	Alex Preston-Jeffreys (5) 76
Scarlett Creasey (6) 45	Grace Humberstone (6) 77
Helen Vrancken (6) 46	Kiran Coomasaru (5) 78
Pierre Gathy (7) 47	Lauren Swallow (6) 79
	Lara Howie (5) 80

Holy Trinity CE Primary School, Woking

Alex Thomas (5) 48	George Peaurt (5) 80
Oliver Baynham (7) 49	Kiera Heney (6) 81
Isabelle Cunningham (7) 50	Libby Jans (5) 81
Eliza Waite (7) 50	Brooke Hibbins (5) 82
William Wieland (6) 51	Jack Bullamore (5) 83
Daniel O'Regan (6) 52	Daisy Richardson (5) 84
Jessica Roles (7) 53	Jessica Franklin (7) 85
Oliver Cooper-Burrows (6) 54	Mia Strong (7) 86
Jacob Gurden (6) 55	Lily Jade Kerr (7) 86
Tilly Phillips (6) 56	Annie Mae Woodward (7) 87
Thomas Robinson (6) 57	Ben Willis (6) 87
Amy Taplin (6) 58	Nathan Everett (6) 88
Ryan Knight (7) 58	Danny Manning (6) 88
Harvey Hewson 59	Ben Gurden (6) 89
Laurence Lisita-Robinson (6) 59	Scott Ross (7) 89
Cameron Fletcher (6) 60	Luca Watson-Hart (7) 90
Oliver Trowbridge (5) 61	Molly Barnard (6) 91
Megan Thomas (6) 62	Jay Jardine (7) 92
Jacob Barker (5) 62	Rose Roberts (6) 92
Lily Kelsey (6) 63	Daniel Davis (6) 93
Max Traylor (5) 63	Kessia Booth (6) 93
	Eloise Bartlett (6) 94
	Faye Hyde (6) 94

Jemma Gregory (6) 95
Grace Carr (7) 95

Homefield Preparatory School, Sutton
Dillon Patel (6) 96
Joel Ajay (6) 96
Oliver Lobb-Rossini (7) 97
Joshua Stearnes (7) 98
Matthew Thomas (7) 99
Callum Jopling (6) 100
Samuel Hoyes (6) 100
Abdullah Baig (5) 101
Benjamin Scott (5) 101
Kiyan Rahman (6) 101
Yusuf Surty (7) 102
Bryn Craske (6) 102
Humphrey Povey (6) 103
Ruairi O'Rourke (6) 103
Adam Hitchens (6) 104
Joe Cronje (7) 104

Meadowcroft Community Infant School, Chertsey
Ralph Irwin (5) 105
Jacob Beszcynski (6) 105
Austin Skeet (5) 105
Tillie Harding (5) 106
Isabel Hoare (5) 106
River Worrall (6) 106
Molly Hazledine (6) 107
George Yeo (6) 107
Kian Baker-Humphreys (6) 108
Fletcher McRae (5) 108
Francis Almonguera (5) 109
Laura White (6) 109

Oakwood School, Oakwood
Raulf Berry (7) 110
Andreas Vlahodimos-Hinton (7) 110
William Hawkins (6) 110
Annabel Heaton (6) 111
Mya Snowdon-Darling (7) 111
Lauren Sutton (6) 112
Joseph Simpson (7) 112
Daniel Colgate (7) 113
Alfie Fisher (7) 113
Olivia Harris (7) 114

Remi Briggs (7) 114
Zara Best (6) 115
Maddison Calvesbert Sharp (6) 115
Broghan Collier (5) 116
Archie Richardson (5) 116
Madeleine Boiardini (5) 117
Poppy Chandler (6) 117
Emily Taylor (5) 118
Oliver Curley (5) 118
Milly Betsworth (6) 119
Francis Palmer (5) 119
Benjamin Cotton (6) 120
Isabel Harris (6) 120
Charlotte Tennant (5) 121
Jonathan Hoskins (5) 121
Nicholas Sampson (5) 122
Rafe Crane-Robinson (4) 122
Cameron Sutherland (5) 123
Henry Harris (4) 123
Amber Street (4) 124
Ruby Chandler (4) 124
Nieve Carson (5) 124

Springfield First School, Worthing
Ryan (6) 125
Kai Nicholas (5) 125
Ben Collins (6) 125
Kai (6) 126
Lewis Cornford (6) 126
Ben Fisher (6) 127
Jessi (6) 127
Adara (6) 128
Sumayyah Nawab (5) 128
Ryan (6) 129
Kimberley Laird (6) 129
Finlay (6) 130
Finlay (6) 130
Lara Mitchell (6) 130
Hannah Callahan (5) 131
Luc Begej (5) 131
Isabella Brady (6) 131
Georgia Stowe (5) 132
Joshua (6) 132
Ethan Daniels (5) 132
Matilda (6) 133

The Weald CE Primary School, Dorking

George Hopper (5) 133
Mia Foskett (4) 133
Emily Mae Fuller (5) 134
Charlie Harris (4) 134
Lola Daniels (5) 135
Mia Cooper (5) 135
Jake Eastwood (5) 135
Lola Watts (5) 136
Noah Jolly (4) 136
Hannah Flashman (4) 136
Ethan Bond (4) 137
Lex McIntosh (4) 137
Ryan Flashman (5) 137
Joshua Thomas (4) 138
Oliver Brien (4) 138

Westfield Primary School, Woking

Miley James (6) 138
Benjamin Lewis 139
Elise Cordery (6) 139
Poppy-Bell Nash (5) 140
Nicole Crick-Marshall (6) 140

The Poems

My First Acrostic 2011 - Sussex & Surrey

Treasure

T reasure is gold and silver.
R ubies shiny and red.
E meralds shiny and green.
A ll jewels shiny.
S ilver coins and rings.
U nder the sand is treasure.
R eally shiny jewels.
E very pirate is happy.

Jemima Goldsmith (5)
Birchwood Grove Community Primary School, Burgess Hill

Pirate

P irates used to sail the seven seas.
I n the old days pirates used to steal treasure.
R ats used to come on the ships.
A ll pirates used to fight.
T reasure is gold and silver.
E very pirate had a day off.

Thomas Penswick (5)
Birchwood Grove Community Primary School, Burgess Hill

Jolly Roger

J olly Roger belongs to a pirate.
O i, ahoy there my ship mates.
L and ahoy.
L ook there is some treasure.
Y es there is treasure, gold and silver coins.

R un away the pirates are coming.
O h no! The pirates are running away with the treasure.
G old and silver coins spill out of the treasure chest.
E veryone picked up the treasure.
R un away to the ship and sail away.

Rebekah Sayle (6)
Birchwood Grove Community Primary School, Burgess Hill

Ahoy There!

A hoy there my ship mate.
H ave you seen the pirates?
O h no the pirates are coming.
Y o ho ho.

T hey are looking for treasure.
H ere is the treasure.
E verybody is happy.
R un to the pirates' ship.
E verybody sing and dance.

Daisy Thring (6)
Birchwood Grove Community Primary School, Burgess Hill

My First Acrostic 2011 - Sussex & Surrey

Captain

C aptain used to wear smart clothes.

A hoy there me hearties.

P arrots sit on a captain's shoulder.

T ime went by.

A nd they sailed the seven seas.

I could see the captain fighting.

N ever upset the captain otherwise you might walk the plank.

Megan Leaney (6)
Birchwood Grove Community Primary School, Burgess Hill

Rats

R ats are crawling around.

A rat was sniffing the pirate's food.

T heir tails were wagging angrily.

S o the pirates came and frightened them away.

Molly Harrild (6)
Birchwood Grove Community Primary School, Burgess Hill

Rats

R ats jumped on board.

A re they eating all the fish?

T ell them to stop.

S top them coming on the ship.

Dylan Boylett (6)
Birchwood Grove Community Primary School, Burgess Hill

Ships

S hips sometimes sank
H unt for some treasure
I n the ship a pirate's sailing
P irates stole the treasure.

Lily Begum (5)
Birchwood Grove Community Primary School, Burgess Hill

Captain

C aptains were cross.
A ll the pirates looking for treasure.
P irates sailed the seven seas.
T he pirates used to find treasure.
A ll the pirates looking for treasure.
I n the ship is a captain.
N ever upset the captain.

Joshua Kerr (6)
Birchwood Grove Community Primary School, Burgess Hill

Parrots

P arrots like to sit on a pirate's shoulder.
A parrot is noisy.
R ats on board.
R ats eat cheese.
O utside the ship are monsters.
T he pirates like drinking tea.

Tabitha Hide Stewart (5)
Birchwood Grove Community Primary School, Burgess Hill

My First Acrostic 2011 - Sussex & Surrey

Ahoy

A pirate sailed the seven seas.
H e had a day off and drank rum.
O h no it is time to sail.
Y o ho ho he found treasure.

Max Spooner (5)
Birchwood Grove Community Primary School, Burgess Hill

Ship

S uddenly rats came on board.
H elp, they have stolen the food.
I can see the pirates are angry.
P irates like their biscuits and rum.

Oliver Hester (6)
Birchwood Grove Community Primary School, Burgess Hill

Ship

S hips sail the seven seas.
H elp there is a pirate!
I can see them looking for treasure.
P irates fight for the gold.

Reuben Kerr (5)
Birchwood Grove Community Primary School, Burgess Hill

Pirates

P irates like sparkly treasure.

I sail the seven seas.

R ats used to come on board.

A nd we had a break.

T ime to stop.

E nd of the journey.

S ail back home to their island.

Jayden Zhang (6)
Birchwood Grove Community Primary School, Burgess Hill

Pirate

P irates have parrots.

I slands are sometimes where they bury treasure.

R igging is for pirates to climb up.

A ye aye Captain.

T reasure maps are for finding treasure.

E ye patches are for pirates to wear.

Daisy Miller (5)
Birchwood Grove Community Primary School, Burgess Hill

My First Acrostic 2011 – Sussex & Surrey

Pirate treasure

T reasure to find.
R igging to climb.
E veryone climb on board.
'A ye aye Captain.'
S ailing boats.
U nder the boat there's fish.
R unning on the deck.
E ach of my mates gets treasure.

Katie O'Toole (5)
Birchwood Grove Community Primary School, Burgess Hill

Pirates

P irate ship
I can fight the other pirates
R ats on board
A ye aye Captain
T reasure to find
E ye patch.

Maddy Stewart-Parsons (5)
Birchwood Grove Community Primary School, Burgess Hill

Pirate Porthole

P ortholes are a ship's window.
O h! There's a man overboard.
R igging to climb.
T reasure to find.
H eavy anchor to pull.
O ur ship has gone.
L ook at the flag.
E ye patch over their eye.

Eleanor Cole (6)
Birchwood Grove Community Primary School, Burgess Hill

Pirate Riggings

R ed beard.
I 'm the captain.
G et on the plank.
G o put the Jolly Roger up.
I will walk the plank.
N one of the crew can play.
G o sail the ship.
S o the ship has sunk.

Katie Hobbs (6)
Birchwood Grove Community Primary School, Burgess Hill

My First Acrostic 2011 - Sussex & Surrey

Pirate's Chest

C utlass to fight.
H eavy anchor.
E veryone climb on board.
S hips to sail in sea.
T reasure map to follow.

Ethan Hall (6)
Birchwood Grove Community Primary School, Burgess Hill

Pirate Riggings

R iggings to climb.
I slands with treasure.
G rey pirates look funny.
G reen and red parrots eat crackers.
I like nice pirates.
N obody likes a bad pirate.
G reen is on a parrot.
S mall pirates can't fight.

Holly Izzard (5)
Birchwood Grove Community Primary School, Burgess Hill

Pirate Treasure

T reasure chest.
R iggings to climb on.
E ye patch on.
'A ye aye Captain!'
S hips sail.
U nder the boat is the anchor.
R unning on the deck.
E veryone climb on board.

Hannah Johanson (5)
Birchwood Grove Community Primary School, Burgess Hill

Pirate Parrot

P irates go on board
A pirate flag
R ig the ship
R ip the flag
O pen the treasure chest
T he ship got in trouble.

Jamie Padgham (6)
Birchwood Grove Community Primary School, Burgess Hill

My First Acrostic 2011 – Sussex & Surrey

Pirate's Treasure

T reasure map to find treasure
R igging to climb
E veryone on board
A nchor to throw
S hip for the sea
U p into the crow's-nest
R ats on board
E ye patch for the captain.

Tallia Clarke (6)
Birchwood Grove Community Primary School, Burgess Hill

Pirate

P ieces of eight
I n the crow's nest
R igging to climb
A ye aye Captain
T reasure to find
E veryone climb on board.

Amelie Palmer-Brown (6)
Birchwood Grove Community Primary School, Burgess Hill

The Ship's Riggings

R ide the ship
I n the ship
G rog to drink
G et the treasure
I am the captain
N o, that's our treasure
G o and get the captain
S hiver me timbers.

Nathan Drake (5)
Birchwood Grove Community Primary School, Burgess Hill

Pirate's Parrot

P irate get on board
A nts on board
R ats on board
R ats on you
O n board
T o get on.

Ryan Goss (5)
Birchwood Grove Community Primary School, Burgess Hill

Treasure For Pirates

T reasure to find
R igging to climb
E veryone on board
A ye aye Captain
S ails make the ship go
U p in the crow's-nest
R ough sea
E ach pirate has a sword.

Mila Anscombe (6)
Birchwood Grove Community Primary School, Burgess Hill

Pirate's Parrot

P irates climb the rigging
A ye aye Captain
R ats on board
R ats at sea
O pen the chest
T reasure to find.

Nathan Ward (5)
Birchwood Grove Community Primary School, Burgess Hill

Rainbow Bear

R ainbow Bear is hunting for the beautiful rainbow.
A n extremely nice man called Shaman.
I love my home.
N ever give up and I will return back to the Arctic.
B eautiful rainbow soaked me into rainbow colours.
O pposite me I saw Shaman.
W hen I was in a cage a bow rescued me hurray!

B rilliant colours shocked me.
E scaped from the cage.
A horrible cage to live in.
R ainbow Bear has extremely soft fur.

Isobel Cooper (7)
Birchwood Grove Community Primary School, Burgess Hill

Pirate Sword

S harp and pointy.
W ent to sea.
O ut come the eyes!
R ip the skin.
D ead pirates.

Joel Cragg (5) & Jack Smart (6)
Birchwood Grove Community Primary School, Burgess Hill

My First Acrostic 2011 - Sussex & Surrey

Pirate Treasure

T housands of jewels.
R eally jealous.
E ach pirate has a turn.
A lot of treasure.
S hiver me timbers!
U p goes the Jolly Roger.
R eady to fight.
E very pirate finds treasure.

Thomas Johnson & Louis White (5)
Birchwood Grove Community Primary School, Burgess Hill

Rainbow Bear

R ainbow Bear is beautiful because he is stripy.
A man was fishing in the snow.
I nuit man told him to make a wish.
N asty men captured Rainbow Bear.
B eautiful colours on him.
O pen the cage let me out.
W ild white wilderness.

B eautiful soft snow.
E asy to get out of the cage, make a wish.
A nd see dazzling colours of the rainbow.
R aining soft white snow.

Ruby Mayes (7)
Birchwood Grove Community Primary School, Burgess Hill

Rainbow Bear

R ainbows are glistening up in the sky.
A crack in the ice is super dangerous.
I nuits love igloos.
N ight time is beautiful.
B eautiful rainbow is above me.
O wls are hooting by me.
W alrus have sharp tusks.

B ears are running in the deep, deep snow.
E ager to go home.
A day in a cage.
R ainbow is close to me.

Ryan Sargent (7)
Birchwood Grove Community Primary School, Burgess Hill

Rainbow Bear

R acing in the soft snow.
A rctic ice all around.
I n the frosty snow chasing its prey.
N ight polar bear hunts.
B eautiful glittering polar bear.
O h! How could I catch that rainbow?
W inter bear hunts.

B ear hunts for its prey.
E xercising people had a rest.
A polar bear is in a cage.
R ainbow look for the polar bear.

Georgia McLean (6)
Birchwood Grove Community Primary School, Burgess Hill

My First Acrostic 2011 - Sussex & Surrey

Rainbow Bear

R unning in the glistening snow.
A rctic is freezing but I can survive.
I nuits hunt me.
N orth Pole is my home.
B rown walrus stands up against me.
O ften I swim in the frozen water.
W hite is my fur colour.

B rave I am.
E very time I see food, I pounce on it.
A rctic foxes are fast.
R ainbow bear.

Benjamin Pryse (7)
Birchwood Grove Community Primary School, Burgess Hill

Rainbow Bear

R ainbow Bear is graceful.
A bear is all alone on the snow.
I want to catch my prey.
N o one is around me.
B ig walrus is too big to eat.
O h I am a rainbow bear, I miss being a white bear.
W hen will someone rescue me?

B eautiful colours of the rainbows around me.
E ek I saw some people coming to eat me.
A nother seal but it bit me on the nose.
R ainbow bears are not so great after all.

Amy Kenward (7)
Birchwood Grove Community Primary School, Burgess Hill

Rainbow Bear

Rainbow Bear has extremely soft fur.
An extremely kind man talks to Rainbow Bear.
I got caught in a net.
Nasty men captured me.
Beautiful rainbow came back and rescued me.
Open the cage and let me out.
Wonderful white wilderness.

Beautiful blue sea.
Even the inuits are cold.
A beautiful day.
Rainbow Bear is one leap away from the rainbow.

Hannah Jellett (7)
Birchwood Grove Community Primary School, Burgess Hill

Rainbow Bear

Rainbow Bear is colourful.
A bear all alone on the soft white snow.
I am Rainbow Bear.
Nothing is the same without my white fur.
Being in my wild wilderness is my favourite place.
Only me, so lonely.
When will someone rescue me?

Being a polar bear is lovely.
Everyone can see me because I'm not white.
All is the same with my white fur.
Rainbow coloured bears are beautiful.

Alex Pilbeam (7)
Birchwood Grove Community Primary School, Burgess Hill

My First Acrostic 2011 – Sussex & Surrey

Rainbow Bear

R ainbow Bear didn't want to be a white bear,
A ll he wanted was to be a rainbow bear.
I t was nice at first to be a rainbow bear,
N ice to roll in the snow.
B ut it wasn't good to be a rainbow bear,
O nly white things can camouflage in the snow.
W hen the hunters came they caught Rainbow Bear.

B oys and girls came to see Rainbow Bear,
E veryone liked him.
A boy saved him,
R ainbow Bear wasn't a rainbow bear anymore.

Tristan Hepburn (7)
Birchwood Grove Community Primary School, Burgess Hill

Rainbow Bear

R ainbow Bear is hunting for the bright beautiful rainbow.
A n extremely wise Inuit told the bear the rainbow word is a wish.
I got put in a net and got taken away from my home.
N ight and day I was kept in that extremely horrifying cage.
B rilliantly tasty seals slipping on the ice.
O h bother I am really tired of this cage.
W hy do seals go fast in the sea so I can't catch them?

B rilliant lovely white snow.
E very day in my white home is great.
A lovely white day in my lovely wilderness.
R ight away I sped on the snow but they caught me.

Harry Heath (6)
Birchwood Grove Community Primary School, Burgess Hill

Rainbow Bear

R olling polar bears.
A nimals live there.
I can see snowballs.
N o dogs or sledges.
B e very cold.
O range in the night.
W indy ice in the snow.

B ees do not live there.
E xplorers hunt for polar bears.
A mazing creatures.
R unning and tumbling in the snow.

Jake Trist (7)
Birchwood Grove Community Primary School, Burgess Hill

Rainbow Bear

R unning polar bears.
A running polar bear.
I can see a polar bear.
N o dogs or sleds.
B e very careful.
O h no.
W hoops.

B eware.
E at up polar bears.
A rgh!'
R un.

Mark Jellett (7)
Birchwood Grove Community Primary School, Burgess Hill

My First Acrostic 2011 – Sussex & Surrey

Rainbow Bear

R olling down the hill going fast
A mazing polar bears
I can see the polar bears playing
N aughty cubs polar bears
B ears do you know if they have a bath?
' O w,' said the polar bear
W e will watch the polar bears

B ig polar bears
E at up polar bear!
A polar bear is rolling down the hill
R oar goes the polar bear.

Harry Argles & Toby Lewis (7)
Birchwood Grove Community Primary School, Burgess Hill

Rainbow Bear

R unning polar bear.
A lot of snowballs.
I see a snowmobile.
N o dogs or sledges.
B e very careful.
O h no!
W hoa!

B ye bye polar bear.
E at, eat, eat.
A n igloo for shelter.
R olling polar bear.

Samuel Biss (6)
Birchwood Grove Community Primary School, Burgess Hill

Rainbow Bear

R oaring bear.
A snowy mountain where a polar bear sat down.
I n an icy land.
N aughty cubs fight.
B aby bears are kind.
O h how cold it is.
W ow it is very cold.

B addy bears attack.
E very polar bear is white.
A polar bear is stalking.
R are polar bears.

Max Blanthorn (6)
Birchwood Grove Community Primary School, Burgess Hill

Rainbow Bear

R oaring bear moving
A cross the ice
I n an icy frozen land
N ext he climbed up the mountain
B addies are attacking him
O h how cold it is
W ow it's very cold

B aby bears are tired
E very polar bear is white
A polar bear loves swimming
R unning down a snowy hill.

James Rose (7)
Birchwood Grove Community Primary School, Burgess Hill

My First Acrostic 2011 - Sussex & Surrey

Rainbow Bear

R ainbow Bear leaps.
A polar bear is enormous.
I can see a polar bear.
N ever before I saw a polar bear.
B ouncing up high.
O ver the sky he goes.
W indy but he still keeps going.

B ear is snowy
E very polar bear is white
A bear is asleep
R unning in the cold snow.

Lucy McNiven (6)
Birchwood Grove Community Primary School, Burgess Hill

Rainbow Bear

R ainbow Bear leaps
A polar bear is digging
I can see a polar bear
N ever before I have seen one
B ouncing hares, bouncing high
O ver the hill there the seals are
W indy weather in the North Pole

B ear is cute
E very polar bear is white
A ttacking polar bear
R unning very fast.

Emma Wickens (6)
Birchwood Grove Community Primary School, Burgess Hill

Rainbow Bear

R olling down the sparkling hill
A mazing animals watching it
I ce melting very slowly
N ow it's very quiet
B ouncing up and down
O n a sunny day
W hite glistening snow

B eware of slips
E choing
A mazing echoes that I can hear
R unning in the cold snow.

Stephanie Zhou (6)
Birchwood Grove Community Primary School, Burgess Hill

The Arctic

A polar bear is wild.
R eindeer galloping in the glistening snow.
C lever polar bears climbing in the snow.
T he polar bears are hunting.
I ce really melting fast.
C unning fox hunting the prey.

Michael Lea (6)
Birchwood Grove Community Primary School, Burgess Hill

My First Acrostic 2011 - Sussex & Surrey

Bird

B urping
I rritating
R ed
D uck.

George Goldsmith (7)
Bosham Primary School, Bosham

Cat

C ute
A ngelic
T ired.

India Rose (7)
Bosham Primary School, Bosham

Mollie The Mouse

M ollie
O ld
U nderground
S queaky
E eky.

Mollie Clark (6)
Bosham Primary School, Bosham

Hedgehog

H omely
E njoyable
D ancing
G iggly
E xcitable
H ot
O bbly
G olden hedgehog.

Charly Turpin (6)
Bosham Primary School, Bosham

Penguin

P erfect penguin
E asy to beat
N osey, beware
G iggly too
U gly so don't be near
I nvisible, he will be invisible to you
N ice, you would like him.

Olivia Toms (7)
Bosham Primary School, Bosham

My First Acrostic 2011 - Sussex & Surrey

Dog

D igging
O ld
G rubby.

Tayla Heron (6)
Bosham Primary School, Bosham

Sunshine

S unshine is bright.
U nder the ground you grow.
N ew.
S eeds.
H igh in the sky are aeroplanes.
I n the sky I see clouds.
N ight is when everyone is asleep.
E lephants are big and heavy.

Joshua Maisuria-Hull (5)
Danesfield Manor School, Walton-on-Thames

Luminous

L ights are bright in the night.
U p in the sky.
M ummy wants to go to space.
I n the house it is quiet.
N ight is dark.
O utside in the darkness it is scary.
U s in our bed all tucked up.
S tars twinkling in the sky.

Saskia Lawrence (6)
Danesfield Manor School, Walton-on-Thames

Moon

M ummy and me like the dark
O ver there we look
O ver the moon and it is very good
N ow.

Isabella Smith (5)
Danesfield Manor School, Walton-on-Thames

Sun

S pace is dark
U p comes the sun
N ow there is a fight.

Louis MacDonald (6)
Danesfield Manor School, Walton-on-Thames

My First Acrostic 2011 – Sussex & Surrey

Firework

F ireworks are shining in the sky.
I watch the fireworks at night.
R ockets are fun.
E verybody likes fireworks.
W ork on the moon is fun.
O ranges are nice.
R ain is the kindest friend.
K atie sent me an email.

Kaya Kondel (5)
Danesfield Manor School, Walton-on-Thames

Annabel

A ll of my family are nice and great.
N ice mummy brings me good things to eat after school.
N ice Daddy takes me for a walk with my dog, Henry.
A eroplanes take us to Dubai.
B eing with my friends for tea is fun!
E mily is my sister and she plays with me.
L aetitia is my friend at school, she is blonde.

Annabel Pilgrim (4)
Danesfield Manor School, Walton-on-Thames

Zachary

Zips go up and down
Apples are green and red
Caterpillars have lots of feet
Horses can run all day
Ants are very tiny
Robots talk and walk funny
Yaks have horns and look like bulls.

Zachary Smith (4)
Danesfield Manor School, Walton-on-Thames

Emily

Everyone loves me and I love them
Mummy gives me sweets, sometimes!
I love counting numbers.
Laetitia is my friend at school.
Yellow is my favourite colour.

Emily Hewens (4)
Danesfield Manor School, Walton-on-Thames

Day

Daddy is good at apple bobbing.
A house is big.
Yoda is a master at Star Wars.

Samuel Clough (5)
Danesfield Manor School, Walton-on-Thames

My First Acrostic 2011 – Sussex & Surrey

Sunshine

S tars go away.
U p comes the sun.
N ow it's daytime.
S un shines.
H ot summer.
I have an ice cream.
N ow I have fun.
E veryone is happy.

Thomas White (5)
Danesfield Manor School, Walton-on-Thames

Laetitia

L adybirds fly in the sky.
A pples are nice colours.
E verything makes me smile.
T oys from Father Christmas are nice.
I love my teachers at school.
T hings I like best are my cuddly toys.
I listen to music and like to sing to it.
A ll of my friends are special.

Laetitia Clift (4)
Danesfield Manor School, Walton-on-Thames

Himmat

H aving my friends around for tea is nice.
I like having chips for my tea.
M y mummy is a good cook.
M y daddy is big and strong.
A ll of my family are good.
T alking to my brother and sisters is fun.

Himmat Bains (4)
Danesfield Manor School, Walton-on-Thames

Bailey

B oys like to play football.
A ll of my family are kind.
I like to watch football with my daddy.
L ovely food is nice.
E verybody I play with is my friend.
Y oghurts are yummy.

Bailey MacDonald (4)
Danesfield Manor School, Walton-on-Thames

Theo

T he best thing about school is seeing my friends.
H elping my teacher with special jobs.
E verybody is nice.
O pening presents is fun, fun, fun.

Theo Marshall (4)
Danesfield Manor School, Walton-on-Thames

My First Acrostic 2011 – Sussex & Surrey

Robert

R abbits are fluffy and I like them
O livia is my baby sister and she likes to cry
B ut I help look after her
E verybody is coming to my party
R iding my bike is fun, fun, fun
T oys are my favourite things.

Robert Russell (4)
Danesfield Manor School, Walton-on-Thames

Winter

W inter is when fierce winds come and snowflakes fall from the sky.
I ce turns to water as it gets warmer.
N ights get longer in the winter so it gets dark earlier.
T he deciduous trees are bare in the winter.
E verything gets covered in frost during winter.
R ed berries, lights, Christmas and wreaths.

Ria Kishani Jayawardene (7)
Danesfield Manor School, Walton-on-Thames

Ahan

A rav is my brother, he likes to play with me
H aving pasta makes me happy
A fter school I play football
N anny lives far away in India!

Ahan Sinha (5)
Danesfield Manor School, Walton-on-Thames

Christmas

C hristmas is a time of year when it gets colder and children get loads of presents.

H ark the Herald Angels sing is a Christmas carol.

R eindeer come at Christmas on Santa's sleigh.

I love Christmas because I get lots of Christmas presents.

S anta comes at Christmas to all the good children around the world.

T itanic is one of the movies I watched at Christmas.

M ary and Joseph went to Bethlehem on Christmas Eve.

A t Christmas I go on holiday and go to church.

S tars glow at Christmas.

Nicole Farmer (6)
Danesfield Manor School, Walton-on-Thames

Snowflakes

S now falls at Christmas time.

N ights get longer in the winter and they also get darker.

O n very cold days snowflakes fall from the clouds.

W inter is a very cold time of year.

F lakes fall when it is very cold and the garden will be covered in snow.

L ater in the winter the weather gets warmer

A s you touch it.

K eep warm with a water bottle.

E very winter Father Christmas comes!

Madeleine White (6)
Danesfield Manor School, Walton-on-Thames

My First Acrostic 2011 – Sussex & Surrey

Giraffie

G iraffes eat leaves off trees and they have orange spots.
I n the desert you can find
R ocks on the sand.
A strong long graceful neck so
F emale giraffes are beautiful.
F unky giraffes moving their necks back and forward.
I have got a toy giraffe at home.
E nd of the day giraffes go to sleep.

Helena O'Neill (7)
Danesfield Manor School, Walton-on-Thames

Pirates

P irates are sea robbers and sailing men.
I slands to find pirate treasure!
R obbers are so bad.
A ll pirates were nasty.
T hey kidnap as well as stealing.
E very pirate does something bad.
S o never turn into a pirate!

Max Culpin (7)
Danesfield Manor School, Walton-on-Thames

Fantastic Mr Fox

F oxes are fantastic.
A ll rabbits are cute.
N annies like knitting.
T aps are stinky when they become dirty.
A ctors are very good at acting.
S am loves watching TV.
T he leaves on the trees in autumn.
I like Fantastic Mr Fox.
C ats are afraid of dogs.

M r Fox is a good character,
R arely children get to stay up late.

F luffy candyfloss yummy in my tummy.
O tters like foxes.
X boxes are for foxes.

Samuel Wells (6)
Danesfield Manor School, Walton-on-Thames

My First Acrostic 2011 – Sussex & Surrey

Dancing

D ad and Mum dance together
A nika dancing to the music
N ana boogies
C akes for energy when you dance.
I like to dance on the Wii.
N oisy music and laughing.
G ood fun dancing!

Anika Pintos-Cummings (6)
Danesfield Manor School, Walton-on-Thames

Ocean

O ctopus has eight legs.
C rabs can snap.
E verywhere fish and other animals.
A shark eats fish.
N ibbling our toes.

Jacques Behier (6)
Danesfield Manor School, Walton-on-Thames

Christmas

C louds fill up the sky as snow falls.
H appy celebrations happen at Christmas and Santa Claus comes.
R ed berries on holly bushes.
I ce skating and skiing.
S inging Christmas songs is peaceful and calm.
T rees being put up to be decorated.
M aking Christmas decorations is fun.
A corns and berries on wreaths.
S tars shine bright in the winter sky.

Isabella Coro (7)
Danesfield Manor School, Walton-on-Thames

Kinect

K inect comes with four games.
I t is amazing, good and wonderful.
N o mics in Kinect for Xbox.
E veryone can play.
C an I play on Xbox.
T his is fun!

Benjamin David Fish (6)
Danesfield Manor School, Walton-on-Thames

My First Acrostic 2011 - Sussex & Surrey

Happy

H ard crisp carrots to crunch.
A laughing dolphin.
P eanuts salty and plain.
P ackets of sweets.
Y ummy in my tummy!

Jamie McNeill (6)
Danesfield Manor School, Walton-on-Thames

France

F romage is the French word for cheese
R ouge, blanc and blue is the French flag
   which is called the drapeau tricolore.
A eroplanes take one hour to get from France to England.
N ice is where my cousin lives.
C aux is where my French grandma lives and grandpa.
E iffel Tower is one of the tallest towers in the world.

Alexandre Lucas (7)
Danesfield Manor School, Walton-on-Thames

In Football

I n football you kick balls.
N o football players can kick you.

F ootball players sometimes get red cards.
O pen football matches are big.
O n the shoes are many studs.
T errific goals are scored.
B ig players can hurt little football players.
L adies watch football matches.
L ots of people come to watch.

Emilia Cavanagh (6)
Danesfield Manor School, Walton-on-Thames

Winter

W ind is blowing across the cloudy sky.
I cy puddles freezing on the hard concrete.
N aughty boys throwing snowballs at chilly people.
T rickling drops of water dripping from melting icicles on the roof.
E xcited children building lumpy snowmen.
R oaring wind blowing across the western sky.

Claudia Platts (6)
Hall Grove School, Bagshot

My First Acrostic 2011 – Sussex & Surrey

Zoom Rocket Zoom

S hooting stars were hitting the rocky moon.
H uge meteors were zapping through the gloomy sky.
O range stars were whizzing past the glowing moon.
O range sparkles were flying through the dusty sky.
T ravelling aliens were spinning past swirling Saturn.
I ron spaceships were gliding past red Mars.
N inja aliens were hitting dark Pluto.
G rumbling aliens were flying to Planet Earth.

Max Tenenbaum (7)
Hall Grove School, Bagshot

Dolphin Poem

D olphins' tails splash in the sea.
O ver the horizon in the shading sun.
L ooking for fish in the shimmering sea.
P laying with a ball.
H opping on their tails, then home for tea.
I n time for a nice warm bath.
N ight falls over the horizon.
S hh - dolphins are now asleep.

Millie Padfield (6)
Hall Grove School, Bagshot

Spaceship

S pace astronauts gliding through the air.
P lanets all around everywhere.
A steroids floating around.
C raters deep down.
E arth twisting and twisting around.
S aturn moving around the sun.
H igh up in space all is calm.
I n space there are shooting stars.
P erhaps I will go there one day.

Charlie Wyatt (6)
Hall Grove School, Bagshot

Space - I'm The Moon

S pace, I look below and see the human race,
P erhaps I might be a full moon tonight.
A cross the planets and stars astronauts travel,
C omets are darting past me as I fly, through the night sky.
E ven the stars are twinkling goodbye.

Elea Tulloch (7)
Hall Grove School, Bagshot

My First Acrostic 2011 - Sussex & Surrey

Space

S hining stars so far.
P lanets going around and around.
A liens being naughty on the moon.
C lever astronauts flying.
E nergetic rockets flying to space.

Owen Young (6)
Hall Grove School, Bagshot

Toybox

T oday I am going to play with my toy.
O h what joy.
Y ou might like to play with me today.
B ring your toys and let's fly away.
O h what joy it brings me.
X -Men are the best for Billy.

Billy Easeman (6)
Hall Grove School, Bagshot

Space Alien

A stronauts bobbing on the dusty moon
L aunching rockets into space
I 've seen the shiny stars in the dark night sky
E veryone wants to see a crazy comet
N ever go to the sun because it will burn your tongue.

Emily Myers (7)
Hall Grove School, Bagshot

Tiger

T errific tigers are the biggest cats.
I ncredible teeth to kill their prey.
G igantic leaps to go far.
E xcelllent eyesight for seeing in the dark.
R arely make a sound to catch their prey.

Manu Prasad (7)
Hall Grove School, Bagshot

My First Acrostic 2011 – Sussex & Surrey

Planets

P eople watch the rocket blast into space
L et's explore the moon!
A stronauts are lucky
N obody can hear them
E arth looks really round and big
T winkling stars in the sky
S pace has no gravity.

Archie Graham (6)
Hall Grove School, Bagshot

Space Shuttle

S hooting stars rush through the sky
P lanets glide slowly by
A liens bobbing all day long
C raters on the moon big and small
E arth looks like a giant ball.

Scarlett Creasey (6)
Hall Grove School, Bagshot

Shetland Pony

S hetland ponies are fun
H ungry all the time
E ating all day
T hey are cute and
L ove going out for rides
A lways looking for treats
N ibbling at your pockets
D on't give them any crisps

P addocks are where ponies live
O r in stables
N uzzles up to their friend
Y ummy food for ponies.

Helen Vrancken (6)
Hall Grove School, Bagshot

My First Acrostic 2011 - Sussex & Surrey

Space Craft

S aturn's red ring is zooming round and round
P luto is frozen deep in space
A red ball in the sky is Mars
C raters on Jupiter are enormous
E arth is the only planet with life on it

C aves are very rare on Uranus
R ocky Venus is spinning around the sun
A sausage will sizzle fast on Mercury
F ar away out there is Neptune
T he rocket visits them all.

Pierre Gathy (7)
Hall Grove School, Bagshot

This Is Me

A lex is my name
L ove my mummy
E yes are blue
X tra helpings of food

T his is my homework
H as nice teeth
O h no, I have eczema
M y sister's name is Cassie
A s this is Alex
S uper scooter fan.

Alex Thomas (5)
Holy Trinity CE Primary School, Woking

My First Acrostic 2011 - Sussex & Surrey

All About Oliver

O liver B is a boy
L ives in West End
I nterested in sports
V ery good at tennis
E njoys playing football
R eads a lot.

B asketball is a favourite
A mazed at dinosaurs
Y oghurts he likes eating
N oisy sometimes
H ates potatoes
A lways on the go
M akes lots of things.

Oliver Baynham (7)
Holy Trinity CE Primary School, Woking

All About Me

I am fast at running
Super at eating
Amelie is my sister
Blue is the colour of my eyes
Eggs make me poorly
Loves to play
Lives in West End
Enjoy my poem.

Isabelle Cunningham (7)
Holy Trinity CE Primary School, Woking

Eliza

Eliza lives in West End.
Likes jumping up and down.
Is friends with lots of children.
Zooms around on her bike.
Arrives home with a smile.

Eliza Waite (7)
Holy Trinity CE Primary School, Woking

The Noisy Footballer

Wants to score goals
Is a Chelsea fan
Likes the blues
Loves football
Is a Cougars' player
At most games
Match hungry

Wanted to be a pilot
Intelligent
Energetic
Likes pizza
A noisy object
Nicknamed 'the horse'
Doesn't like dancing.

William Wieland (6)
Holy Trinity CE Primary School, Woking

Daniel O'Regan

D aniel likes to play sport.
A ctually rugby is his favourite.
N ice to play with others.
I nterested in football too.
E xcited to be starting Beavers.
L ikes to play games.

O ften looks at books.
R eads really well.
E ats Thai food.
G ives lovely smiles.
A nxious to please.
N aughty sometimes.

Daniel O'Regan (6)
Holy Trinity CE Primary School, Woking

My First Acrostic 2011 - Sussex & Surrey

Jessica Roles

J essica Roles is in year 2.
E xcited at Christmas in Ireland.
S at on a plane to fly over there.
S now caused a long delay.
I nterested in pets.
C at called Ginger at Nana and Papa's.
A hug can calm her down.

R ides on a pony called William.
O llie Otters is where she swims.
L ikes playing on computers.
E njoys tennis with preschool friends.
S nacks on nuts.

Jessica Roles (7)
Holy Trinity CE Primary School, Woking

Oliver Cooper

O liver loves his mum lots
L ollipops are his favourite
I ce skating is wicked
V ery interested in fossils
E very day he is happy
R ugby is the best

C ooler Than Me is his favourite song
O ften he is cheeky
O ranges are yummy
P eople think he's funny
E njoys cricket so much
R eally likes sweets.

Oliver Cooper-Burrows (6)
Holy Trinity CE Primary School, Woking

My First Acrostic 2011 - Sussex & Surrey

Jacob Gurden

J umping is my favourite thing,
A nd I am good at it.
C inemas are fun.
O utside I play football.
B uzzy bees make me run.

G inger and TJ are my cats,
U nder the table they hide.
R ight before bedtime,
D ad or Mummy read me a story.
E very time I cry my eyes leak.
N ight time I cuddle Snuggle Bear.

Jacob Gurden (6)
Holy Trinity CE Primary School, Woking

All About Tilly

M y name is Matilda
A nd I like to play
T eddies are my favourite toy
I enjoy cuddles
L ittle Long Legs is the name of my favourite teddy
D ogs are nice too
A ll animals I love

P olar bears, penguins, I like them all
H ardly any animals are horrible
I nsects aren't very cuddly
L ollipops I like
L icking them a lot
I ncluding candyfloss
P ineapples I like too
S isters are annoying, says my brother.

Tilly Phillips (6)
Holy Trinity CE Primary School, Woking

My First Acrostic 2011 – Sussex & Surrey

About Thomas

T homas is good at karate
H as two guinea pigs called Lily and Rosie
O ctanauts is his favourite programme
M ost favourite birds are blue tits
A wakes in the night
S low as a tortoise

R eads a lot
O n Saturdays plays on the computer
B en 10 is his best game
I nterested in non-fiction books
N oisy
S ensitive
O ff school two days
N ever been on an aeroplane.

Thomas Robinson (6)
Holy Trinity CE Primary School, Woking

All About Me

A qua is my favourite colour
M illy is my best friend
Y ellow is my school table

T akes care of teddies
A pples are my favourite fruit
P laying the recorder is fun
L earning about Mexico is great
I like hot chocolate and chocolate
N eeds lots of cuddles.

Amy Taplin (6)
Holy Trinity CE Primary School, Woking

All About Me

R eally likes football
Y ellow is the colour of his school uniform
A rsenal are his favourite team
N eeds help with homework sometimes

K nows a lot about sport
N ever stops talking
I s in Year 2
G uildford Road is where he lives
H oly Trinity is his school
T hinks his mummy and daddy are ace.

Ryan Knight (7)
Holy Trinity CE Primary School, Woking

My First Acrostic 2011 – Sussex & Surrey

Harvey Hewson

H arvey is seven years old.
A mazing at football.
R eally likes X Factor.
V ery sporty.
E njoys tennis.
Y et hates losing.

H as two younger brothers.
E ats fish fingers.
W ent to Holy Trinity School.
S ends letters to people sometimes.
O n Thursday he goes to PSR.
N ever goes shopping.

Harvey Hewson
Holy Trinity CE Primary School, Woking

Laurence

L ikeable Laurence loves swimming
A nd jumping in the pool
U sually, he goes with his friends
R arely swims on his own
E njoys stroking his cats
N agging his mum to
C lear up his mess in his room
E ven when he's doing nothing!

Laurence Lisita-Robinson (6)
Holy Trinity CE Primary School, Woking

All About Cameron

C ameron is a Scottish name.

A pples I really like, pears too.

M anchester United are my favourite team.

E at my favourite food, fish and chips.

R ugby is what I play on Sundays.

O n Mondays, I go to Beavers.

N ew Zealand is where I come from.

F ootball is my favourite sport.

L achie is my brother.

E ggs I don't like.

T ennis I really enjoy.

C elebrate my birthday in June.

H ave friends called William and James.

E ach day I go to Holy Trinity School.

R eally like golf and skiing.

Cameron Fletcher (6)
Holy Trinity CE Primary School, Woking

My First Acrostic 2011 – Sussex & Surrey

Oliver Trowbridge

O ranges are good for me
L ollies are yummy
I like big sweets
V ery chocolatey
E ating very good
R ugby I can play

T uesday I played tennis
R iding my bike today
O pening presents at Christmas
W alking my dog
B ouncing on my trampoline
R acing my sister
I ce skating on ice
D riving my go-kart fast
G oing shopping with Mummy
E ggs are yummy too.

Oliver Trowbridge (5)
Holy Trinity CE Primary School, Woking

Megan Thomas

M agnificent reader
E njoys gymnastics
G ood at football
A lways tries hard at maths
N eat handwriting

T errific at spellings
H elpful at home
O utstanding at spellings
M arvellous with electricity
A lways eat my dinner
S ensible at home.

Megan Thomas (6)
Holy Trinity CE Primary School, Woking

Dinosaurs

D angerous dinosaurs
I love dinosaurs
N asty big teeth
O phthalmasurus diving in
S plash!
A rchaeopteryx is the size of a chicken
U nlike the gigantic T-rex
R oar! Run away!
S cary, scary Jurassic period.

Jacob Barker (5)
Holy Trinity CE Primary School, Woking

My First Acrostic 2011 – Sussex & Surrey

Lily Kelsey

L ily loves animals.
I ncluding cats, dogs and horses.
L ucky me, I have guinea pigs.
Y es, I have two guinea pigs.

K elsey is my surname.
E misa is my friend.
L isa is my mum.
S weets are yummy.
E veryone likes sweets.
Y esterday I ate lots.

Lily Kelsey (6)
Holy Trinity CE Primary School, Woking

Max Traylor

M y name is Max
A pples are my favourite
X box is what I want

T ries to be faster than Ethan
R eally interested in science
A lways loves Mum
Y oung and good looking
L ikes Star Wars
O ften has a hug
R eally likes chocolate.

Max Traylor (5)
Holy Trinity CE Primary School, Woking

My First Acrostic

K eeps smiling
E ager to run
I nterested in playing games
R eally enjoys judo
A ppreciates my friends

C olours pictures
L ikes football
I like my toys
S ings a lot
B rown hair
Y awns a lot in the mornings.

Keira Clisby (6)
Holy Trinity CE Primary School, Woking

Autumn

A mazing fireworks in the air
U nder the leaves hedgehogs hide
T rees are bare and crunchy leaves are on the ground
U mbrellas, hats, scarves and gloves we wear
M ummy makes hot meals
N early time for Christmas.

Hannah Borthwick (6)
Holy Trinity CE Primary School, Woking

My First Acrostic 2011 - Sussex & Surrey

Lucy Herbert

L oves baking
U tterly delicious cakes and biscuits
C ustard creams are her favourite
Y ummy in her tummy

H as lots of friends to play with
E llie is one of them
R unning round the playground
B ouncing balls happily
E verlasting friendship
R acing back to class
T ime to do some work.

Lucy Herbert (5)
Holy Trinity CE Primary School, Woking

All About Lauren Kaye

L auren is lovely.
A nd has a dog called Poppy.
U mbrellas keep me dry.
R eading is my favourite thing.
E ating chocolate makes me happy.
N eed lots of chocolate for sleepovers.

Lauren Kaye (6)
Holy Trinity CE Primary School, Woking

Jessica Allen

J olly and fun
E njoys playing at home
S ometimes goes to school
S miles when tickled
I s good at drawing
C an run really fast
A rgues with her brother

A fraid of the dark
L oves her family
L earns how to write at school
E ats all of her dinner
N ever gives up.

Jessica Allen (5)
Holy Trinity CE Primary School, Woking

Connie

C onnie loves everyone
O ften is happy
N ever naughty
N ever cries
I nterested in maths
E ats sweets.

Connie Carr (5)
Holy Trinity CE Primary School, Woking

My First Acrostic 2011 - Sussex & Surrey

Aimee Gould

A mazing imagination
I nterested in learning
M erry little thing
E xcellent at spelling
E njoys life

G enerous and kind to friends
O ut going and fun to be with
U nderstanding and thoughtful
L oving to her family
D oesn't like worms.

Aimee Gould (6)
Holy Trinity CE Primary School, Woking

Ellie Grace

E asy to play with
L ikes cookery club
L oves her big sister
I s always smiling
E njoys swimming

G ood fun to be with
R emembers to say please and thank you
A lways thinks of others
C an run very fast
E ats lots of chocolate.

Ellie Moore (5)
Holy Trinity CE Primary School, Woking

All About Me

S miles when he's happy
T raining to be a footballer
E ats turkey at Christmas
F un company
A vramov is my surname
N atasha's my sister.

A friendly boy
V ery good at drawing
R ight handed
A lways likes a game
M ummy likes cooking
O liver is my friend
V ery kind to animals.

Stefan Avramov (6)
Holy Trinity CE Primary School, Woking

My First Acrostic 2011 – Sussex & Surrey

The Éloise Acrostic Poem

É loise is seven
L oves brownies
O nly started last week
I s interested in art
S pends time playing with her toys
E njoys reading her books

B allet on a Saturday
A ndrew is her daddy
S ees her friend Abby at the weekend
T eddy is her favourite toy
I nvents her own games
L esley is her mummy
L oves chocolate
E njoys playing chess.

Éloise Bastille (7)
Holy Trinity CE Primary School, Woking

Happy Harriet

H appy
A lways listens in class
R eads her books nicely
R iding horses is her favourite thing
I s very giggly
E ats her dinner nicely
T ries her best at everything

P ractises her spellings
R uns very fast
I s very helpful
C lever
E njoys being with her friends.

Harriet Price (5)
Holy Trinity CE Primary School, Woking

My First Acrostic 2011 - Sussex & Surrey

I Like My Books

I like reading

L earning is fun
I nformation is useful
K nowing how to read
E arns me good marks

M y Harry Potter books are good
Y ou can read them

B orrowing the library books
O r maybe get another one
O r buy it from the shop
K eeping it forever
S oon you will enjoy them too.

Jack Blamire (5)
Holy Trinity CE Primary School, Woking

Jamie Sice

J amie Sice plays games
A bout 1.20m tall
M esses about with his friends
I s very good at playing football
E ats lots of chocolate

S trokes his cat every day
I sn't grumpy
C an always play
E very day he plays the piano.

Jamie Sice (7)
Holy Trinity CE Primary School, Woking

Lottie Loves Pooh Bear

L ottie loves Pooh Bear
O f all the animals dogs are best
T oy Story 3 is her best film
T hree chickens in the garden
I cing cakes is lots of fun
E loise is her friend.

Lottie Jackson (6)
Holy Trinity CE Primary School, Woking

My First Acrostic 2011 – Sussex & Surrey

Caspar Watson-Hart

C ake is my favourite food
A s I eat my lunch my tummy feels full
S o do my family's tummies feel full
P lo Koon's Starfighter is in my room
A ged five
R ight handed on the Wii

W rites neatly
A rt is my favourite activity
T ennis is my favourite sport
S o is football and swimming
O n my DS I can play games
N an is my grandmother
H ot juice is my favourite drink
A l is on Toy Story
R unning is fun
T okyo is in Japan.

Caspar Watson-Hart (5)
Holy Trinity CE Primary School, Woking

Lauren Hawes

L oves Doggy.
A lways smiling.
U ninterested in homework.
R eally likes sweets.
E njoys playing with her toys.
N ever eats Brussels sprouts.

H as brown eyes.
A dores her guinea pig.
W ants to be a vet.
E njoys cycling.
S ometimes naughty.

Lauren Hawes (6)
Holy Trinity CE Primary School, Woking

My First Acrostic 2011 – Sussex & Surrey

About Me

C ares about others
H as a cheeky face
A lways playing tricks
R eally good at karate
L ikes cats
I s a good sportsman
E njoys playing football.

R uns very fast
O ften scores goals
S miles a lot
E nergetic.

Charlie Rose (6)
Holy Trinity CE Primary School, Woking

Harvey Loves To Make Things

H arvey loves to make things
A ll of the time
R eally keen on dogs
V ery good at building anything
E njoys eating crisps
Y ou will find him a good friend.

Harvey Harriss (5)
Holy Trinity CE Primary School, Woking

Alex

A lways happy
L ikes going to the park
E lephant picture is on my kite
X xx I love my family.

Alex Preston-Jeffreys (5)
Holy Trinity CE Primary School, Woking

My First Acrostic 2011 – Sussex & Surrey

Grace Humberstone

G race has blue eyes
R eally pretty
A good friend
C ares about animals
E njoys riding

H er hair is blonde
U sually happy
M akes Mummy happy
B eautiful girl
E ats lots of chocolate
R eally likes colouring
S he is kind
T eatime is yummy
O n time for school
N ever mean
E veryone's friend.

Grace Humberstone (6)
Holy Trinity CE Primary School, Woking

This Is Me

K icks footballs
I s a good boy
R abbits are his favourite animal
A lways has a story at bedtime
N ever eats Brussels sprouts

C hloe and Laura are his sisters
O nly likes a bath with toys
O ften hugs Mummy and Daddy
M arch 17th is his birthday
A ims to do his best
S ix is his next birthday
A lways cuddles his teddies
R uns really fast
U sually eats all his food.

Kiran Coomasaru (5)
Holy Trinity CE Primary School, Woking

My First Acrostic 2011 – Sussex & Surrey

All About Lauren

L auren likes princesses
A lyssa is my best friend
U nicorns are pretty
R eading Princess Poppy is fun
E ating chocolate is fun
N ever say rude words

S linky is my favourite toy
W oody is a cowboy
A nd Bullseye is his horse
L otso the bear is evil
L auren likes watching TV
O scar is Ben's dog
W alking is good for you.

Lauren Swallow (6)
Holy Trinity CE Primary School, Woking

Things That I Like To Do

L ara loves laughing
A nd stories
R eads every night in bed
A lways giggling

H appy when she's talking
O nly stops when she's asleep
W ishes she was a princess
I n a pink castle with
E lliot, Jack, Mummy and Daddy.

Lara Howie (5)
Holy Trinity CE Primary School, Woking

George Peaurt

G eorge
E njoys playing
O utside in the garden
R ugby playing
G eorge
E ats lots of fruit

P leased to play with
E xcited about new toys
A lways playing with Lego
U nder tables and chairs
R eading stories at bedtime
T o stay up late.

George Peaurt (5)
Holy Trinity CE Primary School, Woking

My First Acrostic 2011 - Sussex & Surrey

Kiera Heney

K angaroos are my favourite
I sabelle is my sister
E lephants are big
R eading is fun
A pples are juicy.

H appy when I am outside
E njoys activities
N ice people
E njoying reading books
Y ummy fruit every day.

Kiera Heney (6)
Holy Trinity CE Primary School, Woking

All About Me

L ikes pink
I nsects scare me
B rothers I have two
B utterflies are pretty
Y ear I was born in was 2005

J am on my toast is my favourite
A lways happy
N ana is nice
S chool is fun.

Libby Jans (5)
Holy Trinity CE Primary School, Woking

All About Brooke

B eautiful is Brooke.
R eading is something I like.
O bviously I'm lovely.
O range is a colour I like.
K ind is what I am.
E nthusiastic always.

H appy on all occasions.
I nteresting to be around.
B right and cheerful all the time.
B reezes in.
I ce lollies are a favourite.
N ice mostly always.
S illy all of the time.

Brooke Hibbins (5)
Holy Trinity CE Primary School, Woking

My First Acrostic 2011 – Sussex & Surrey

Jack The Good Footballer

J am is not my favourite
A rguing with my sister is naughty
C hocolate spread is yummy
K ite flying is fun

B iking with my sister Georgia
U p is a really sad movie
L ike playing football
L ike Cameron Gleed
A li is my mummy
M y favourite colour is green
O ranges are nice to eat
R ugby looks good
E ggs are horrible.

Jack Bullamore (5)
Holy Trinity CE Primary School, Woking

Daisy Richardson

D raws nicely.
A lways kind to others.
I s always good.
S upermarket games at home.
Y uyu is my brother.

R eally good at running.
I like to play with friends.
C an play the piano.
H arvey barks all the time.
A fraid of spiders.
R iding my bike is the best.
D resses up as a princess.
S ings all the time.
O ranges are lovely dipped in glucose.
N ana lives next door to us.

Daisy Richardson (5)
Holy Trinity CE Primary School, Woking

All About Me

J umpy at play time
E njoys playing with my pets
S wims every week
S even years old
I nterested in dancing
C urly hair
A rt is my favourite hobby

F unny with my sister
R ebekah is my mummy
A lways singing
N ever naughty
K elvin is my daddy
L oves my family
I ce cream is my favourite
N ice with my friends.

Jessica Franklin (7)
Holy Trinity CE Primary School, Woking

Mia Strong

M akes fairy cakes.
I nterested in Egyptians.
A lways has a smile.

S cooting is the best.
T akes care of my brother.
R uns very fast.
O ffers to help.
N eeds lots of hugs and kisses.
G oing swimming is lots of fun.

Mia Strong (7)
Holy Trinity CE Primary School, Woking

Little Lily Locket

L ittle Lily Locket
I s living in my pocket
L oving all her time there
Y ou might just see her if you stare

K eep her safe, warm and dry
E very minute that goes by
R eally love our time together
R emember her forever.

Lily Jade Kerr (7)
Holy Trinity CE Primary School, Woking

My First Acrostic 2011 - Sussex & Surrey

Annie Mae Woodward

A nnie is seven and likes horse riding
N eeds lots of sleep
N ice and kind to people
I mproving her swimming
E ats all her dinner

M oves her body to music
A lways turning off her brain
E njoys her friends.

Annie Mae Woodward (7)
Holy Trinity CE Primary School, Woking

Ben Willis

B lue is his favourite colour
E ats lots of nuggets
N ever gets to school late

W alks to school on Friday
I mproving on his handwriting
L ollies are his favourite pudding
L ikes riding his scooter
I nterested in football
S wims on a Wednesday.

Ben Willis (6)
Holy Trinity CE Primary School, Woking

Nathan John

N obody is like Nathan
A boy that is unique
T otally crazy
H as the smelliest feet
A lways friends to everyone
N ever says no to a sweet

J elly babies are my favourite
O n the good side
H onest every time
N obody is like Nathan.

Nathan Everett (6)
Holy Trinity CE Primary School, Woking

Danny, That's Me!

D anny really likes Super Mario
A nd would like to be in a Mario game
N ew Super Mario Bros is the name of the game
N ever losing, always the winner!
Y ear 2011, Super Mario champion, that's Danny!

Danny Manning (6)
Holy Trinity CE Primary School, Woking

My First Acrostic 2011 - Sussex & Surrey

Ben Gurden

B en likes playing football,
E ven in the snow.
N uts are very tasty.

G uns are Ben's favourite toys and
U nder the table he hides.
R eally likes playing on the Wii. -
D efinitely Star Wars is best.
E lephants are his favourite animals.
N ever seen one in the wild.

Ben Gurden (6)
Holy Trinity CE Primary School, Woking

Scott's Smarty Pants

S cott is a smarty pants
C hocolate is his favourite food
O h and a lot of ketchup
T hough not always together
T he other things he really loves are

R unning and gymnastics
O ver the pummel horse then
S plits and rings are next
S miling every day.

Scott Ross (7)
Holy Trinity CE Primary School, Woking

Luca Watson-Hart

L ikes Lego
U nderstands a lot
C aspar is my brother
A ged seven

W ii games are fab
A l is on Toy Story 2
T ennis is my favourite sport
S ome football and swimming
O ranges are my favourite fruit
N eeds lots to do
H ot chocolate is my favourite drink
A rt is fun
R unning is fun
T okyo is in Japan.

Luca Watson-Hart (7)
Holy Trinity CE Primary School, Woking

My First Acrostic 2011 - Sussex & Surrey

Molly Barnard

M y favourite animal is a cat.
O n holiday I like to go swimming.
L ion King is my favourite film.
L iving in West End is really good.
Y ellow sun makes me smile.

B en is my favourite boy's name.
A t my nanny and grandad's home I like to play.
R iding my pony Saturn is great.
N icola is my mummy's name.
A pples are my favourite fruit.
R osy, Poppy and Fonzy are my cats' names.
D arren is my daddy's name.

Molly Barnard (6)
Holy Trinity CE Primary School, Woking

Jay Jardine

J ay loves DVDs
A nd arcade grabbers
Y uck to mushy peas

J ay's best friend is Joel
A nd loves Frosties for breakfast
R eady to do anything
D VDs are great to watch
I like the colour orange
N ever bad! Always good
E very Monday I do cooking!

Jay Jardine (7)
Holy Trinity CE Primary School, Woking

Rose

R ose is my name
O h I join in with games
S kirts that I wear at my school
E njoying the work that I do

R unning in the playground at playtime
O h I love swimming too
B allet is a favourite I do
E nergy that I also have
R eally loves books
T eaching my toys at bedtime
S ocks that keep my lovely feet warm at night.

Rose Roberts (6)
Holy Trinity CE Primary School, Woking

My First Acrostic 2011 – Sussex & Surrey

Daniel Davis

D aniel likes Danny
A nd cats
N ow aged six
I n February I am seven
E very day I like to play
L ove Mum

D on't like sprouts
A nd beans
V isits theme parks
I like the log flume
S oaking wet!

Daniel Davis (6)
Holy Trinity CE Primary School, Woking

Kessia Booth

K ind and helpful
E ats apples
S aturdays are my swimming lessons
S leeps to 7 o'clock
I s always happy
A lovely girl

B elieves in fairies
O ctopuses are funny
O ranges are very sweet
T hinks ballet is good
H as a funny sister.

Kessia Booth (6)
Holy Trinity CE Primary School, Woking

Annoying Sister

E verything my sister does is annoying
L oses my toys
O rders me around
I rritates me and my friends
S teals my sweeties
E ven though I love her.

Eloise Bartlett (6)
Holy Trinity CE Primary School, Woking

Faye Hyde's Poem

F aye is a lovely girl at school
A nd at home
Y ou would like me too
E veryone likes my long curly blonde hair

H ide-and-seek is my best game
Y ou can play too
D addy, Mummy and Brogan are my family and I love them
E veryone in my family loves me very, very much.

Faye Hyde (6)
Holy Trinity CE Primary School, Woking

My First Acrostic 2011 - Sussex & Surrey

This Is Me

J am is yummy,
E nergetic.
M ummy is my best friend.
M y favourite book is Aladdin.
A ll my friends were kind to me.

G randma is the best too.
R eading is the best.
E veryone likes my song.
G lad to be in bed right now.
O nly one sister Katelyn.
R abbits are funny.
Y es I have finished my work.

Jemma Gregory (6)
Holy Trinity CE Primary School, Woking

Grace

G race likes ballet
R eally likes to dance
A pples are my favourite fruit
C ares for people
E ats chocolate.

Grace Carr (7)
Holy Trinity CE Primary School, Woking

Dillon Patel

D reaming Manchester United win the World Cup.
I love swimming.
L iving the dream.
L ove Black Eyed Peas.
O ver the top.
N aturally good at football.

P eace and quiet is hard to get.
A wesome days.
T ry to get clever.
E psom College is where I swim.
L oves pets.

Dillon Patel (6)
Homefield Preparatory School, Sutton

Me!

J olly Joel always happy.
O nly liking to be helpful.
E arns a lot of stickers.
L earns a lot in class.

A ccepts everything that people say to him.

Joel Ajay (6)
Homefield Preparatory School, Sutton

My First Acrostic 2011 – Sussex & Surrey

Oliver Lobb Rossini

O ften I play rugby.
L isten to my poem.
I love the school that I go to.
V ideo games are awesome.
E very day I go to school.
R eading is good for your brain and that's why I am clever.

L ego is my favourite toy.
O nce I played at Harlequins.
B irthday is in December.
B edrooms are nice and cosy.

R emember that I am good at rugby.
O liver has a sister.
S ometimes I eat chocolate.
S wimming is fun.
I 'm called Oliver.
N ext year I'm going to be 8.
I love my home.

Oliver Lobb-Rossini (7)
Homefield Preparatory School, Sutton

Me

J olly Joshua
O ver the top Joshua
S houting-out Joshua
H appy all the time Joshua
U sually working
A mazing Joshua

S uper Joshua
T errific Joshua
E ating a lot Joshua
A rtistic Joshua
R unning around Joshua
N oisy Joshua
E xciting Joshua
S uperb Joshua.

Joshua Stearnes (7)
Homefield Preparatory School, Sutton

My First Acrostic 2011 - Sussex & Surrey

Matthew Thomas

M atthew likes football cards.
A lways look for him.
T he best thing on TV is Star Wars.
T he dog is called Cider.
H omefield is the best school.
E njoys TV on big screen.
W hatever Matthew does he enjoys.

T he worst thing on TV is girls' stuff
H orrid Henry is so cool.
O liver is my best friend.
M atthew does not like work.
A New Hope is so cool because it is Star Wars and I love Star Wars.
S aturday and Sunday are the days off.

Matthew Thomas (7)
Homefield Preparatory School, Sutton

Callum Jopling

C allum likes football cards.
A lways I like Star Wars on TV.
L ogan is my brother, he is eight years old.
L ogan does not like rugby.
U sually I like football games.
M y party was at Goals.

J ake is my cousin.
O lly is another of my cousins.
P am is my nana's name.
L ondon is the city I live in.
I n school I go to chess.
N orth is where my nana and grandpa live.
G randpa is called Shanti.

Callum Jopling (6)
Homefield Preparatory School, Sutton

All About Me

S ometimes clever
A lways available
M aybe a little bit quiet
U sually good
E xcellent boy
L ovely work.

Samuel Hoyes (6)
Homefield Preparatory School, Sutton

My First Acrostic 2011 - Sussex & Surrey

All About Me

A n elephant likes me
B rilliant illustrating
D oing lots of work
U sing sticky bits
L aughing with my friends
L ions like me
A friend makes me happy
H e is kind.

Abdullah Baig (5)
Homefield Preparatory School, Sutton

All About Me

B en is a good boy.
E xciting things happen to me.
N ice places I go to.

Benjamin Scott (5)
Homefield Preparatory School, Sutton

All About Me

K icked a ball
I s nice
Y ou can play with him
A nd he does good work
N ow he is nice.

Kiyan Rahman (6)
Homefield Preparatory School, Sutton

Yusuf Surty

Y ou cannot ignore me
U nder any circumstances!
S ssh no talking!
U pright all the time
F air all the time.

S et for anything
U p on everything
R esults very high
T ry my hardest all the time
Y usuf is super.

Yusuf Surty (7)
Homefield Preparatory School, Sutton

My Name

B rilliant boy
R uns a lot
Y oung but clever
N ice and kind.

Bryn Craske (6)
Homefield Preparatory School, Sutton

My First Acrostic 2011 - Sussex & Surrey

This Is Me

H e is very kind
U nbelievably good
M akes no silly noises
P eople love him
H e helps people
R unning about
E very day he has fun
Y ou would like to meet him!

Humphrey Povey (6)
Homefield Preparatory School, Sutton

Me

R unning about
U nder the sun
A bout all day long
I am tired
R echarging my batteries
I am running again.

Ruairi O'Rourke (6)
Homefield Preparatory School, Sutton

Teatime

A ny chocolate Adam will eat
D oesn't like mushrooms to eat
A lways happy yes he is!
M aking Mum give me treats

J am rings, custard creams

H appy, happy yes he is.

Adam Hitchens (6)
Homefield Preparatory School, Sutton

Breaktime

J ust loves playing
O n the adventure playground
E veryone is happy

C limbing up the climbing frame
R ound and round we spin on the wheel
O n the ground we chase and play
N ot hurting anyone
J umping around the playground
E njoy it, it is excellent!

Joe Cronje (7)
Homefield Preparatory School, Sutton

My First Acrostic 2011 - Sussex & Surrey

Ralph

R eading
A pple
L ucky
P op
H appy.

Ralph Irwin (5)
Meadowcroft Community Infant School, Chertsey

Jacob

J azzy
A rchitect
C reative
O utside
B rilliant.

Jacob Beszcynski (6)
Meadowcroft Community Infant School, Chertsey

Austin

A mazing
U nique
S mart
T errific
I mportant
N eat.

Austin Skeet (5)
Meadowcroft Community Infant School, Chertsey

Tillie

T ickly
I ncredible
L ittle
L ively
I ntelligent
E xciting.

Tillie Harding (5)
Meadowcroft Community Infant School, Chertsey

Isabel

I love Mummy
S ad
A ctive
B eautiful
E xplorer
L ovely.

Isabel Hoare (5)
Meadowcroft Community Infant School, Chertsey

River

R esting
I nvisible
V ery clever
E njoys football
R eading.

River Worrall (6)
Meadowcroft Community Infant School, Chertsey

My First Acrostic 2011 – Sussex & Surrey

Molly Eliza

M ind
O nly
L ittle
L ovely
Y oung

E njoy
L augh
I magination
Z est
A ngel.

Molly Hazledine (6)
Meadowcroft Community Infant School, Chertsey

George Yeo

G reedy
E nergy
O wl
R apid
G ood
E xcited

Y oung
E xplorer
O rganised.

George Yeo (6)
Meadowcroft Community Infant School, Chertsey

Kian Baker

K ind
I ncredible
A ngry
N asty

B ouncy
A dventurer
K ing
E xpert
R obot.

Kian Baker-Humphreys (6)
Meadowcroft Community Infant School, Chertsey

Fletcher

F un
L ively
E xpert
T errific
C ool
H ot
E xcellent
R unner.

Fletcher McRae (5)
Meadowcroft Community Infant School, Chertsey

Francis

F riends
R unning
A crobatic
N ice
C alm
I nventor
S afe.

Francis Almonguera (5)
Meadowcroft Community Infant School, Chertsey

Laura White

L azy
A mazing
U nderstanding
R ich
A ward

W icked
H andsome
I magination
T hinking
E xcellent.

Laura White (6)
Meadowcroft Community Infant School, Chertsey

Raulf

R ugby is on Sunday
A n ant is small
U pstairs is a big bedroom
L ambs are cute
F ootball is on Thursday.

Raulf Berry (7)
Oakwood School, Oakwood

Andreas

A rt is my favourite subject
N ight is my favourite time of day
D ogs look fantastic
R oses are beautiful, I have three
E ggs I don't like at all
A nimals are good
S leepy my dog is.

Andreas Vlahodimos-Hinton (7)
Oakwood School, Oakwood

Bella

B ella is my dog
E xtremely fast when she runs
L icks my face and chases my cat
L aughing when Bella chews my homework
A dventurous, she has been under the decking in the garden.

William Hawkins (6)
Oakwood School, Oakwood

My First Acrostic 2011 – Sussex & Surrey

Annabel

A my is my best friend
N eil is my mummy's friend
N ight time is the time for DVDs
A t night time it is time to sleep
B edtime is the time to dream
E very day at the weekend I pick roses
L adybirds are my favourite insects.

Annabel Heaton (6)
Oakwood School, Oakwood

Mya Snowdon

M y favourite is photography
Y oyos are my favourite
A dog is my best animal

S now is my best weather
N ight I don't like!
O ranges are yuck!
W ales is part of the war
D an is one of the children
O lives are yuck!
N early always I love drawing.

Mya Snowdon-Darling (7)
Oakwood School, Oakwood

Lauren

L ilac is my favourite colour.
A nnabel is my best friend.
U p in the sky is good.
R ed is my favourite colour too.
E lephants are the best.
N ight is the best bit.

Lauren Sutton (6)
Oakwood School, Oakwood

Pompey

P ompey are my favourite team
O ffside is bad
M en are fun
P arties are great
E vents are fun
Y oyos are fun to play with.

Joseph Simpson (7)
Oakwood School, Oakwood

My First Acrostic 2011 - Sussex & Surrey

Daniel

D ogs are cute.
A nimals are interesting.
N erver come in my room.
I n fact I am cool.
E ating is fun, I like eating pasta.
L ying down is boring.

Daniel Colgate (7)
Oakwood School, Oakwood

Chelsea

C helsea is my favourite team
H amsters are cuddly
E ggs are smelly
L ooking after my dog is fun
S ister called Isla who can be cheeky
E ating cauliflower is yummy
A camping holiday with my friends is exciting.

Alfie Fisher (7)
Oakwood School, Oakwood

Olivia

O lives are my yummy thing
L emons are yummy in my house
I have two brothers
V iolet is my cousin
I nvited friends are coming to my party
A nimals are lovely.

Olivia Harris (7)
Oakwood School, Oakwood

World War Two

W ar is a dangerous thing
O rdered to fight other countries
R ussia used to win
L ong, dark, noisy nights
D angerous machines that can kill people.

W indows blacked out
A mazing guns and bombs
R aiding the night sky.

T owers were bombed
W aves of bombers circled the sky
O ur soldiers died for us.

Remi Briggs (7)
Oakwood School, Oakwood

My First Acrostic 2011 - Sussex & Surrey

Birds Eggs

B irds fly
I see eggs
R eal fast flyers
D elicate beaks
S pecial birds.

E at worms
G reat birds
G ood food
S piky feathers.

Zara Best (6)
Oakwood School, Oakwood

Dawdling

D an has gone to dawdling land;
A lways someone dawdling,
W here dawdling is always found,
D an is always there doing some more . . .
L and ahoy there me hearty almost there,
I an is ahead there at least we are back,
N athan is so funny,
G ordon we are almost there.

Maddison Calvesbert Sharp (6)
Oakwood School, Oakwood

Treasure

T reasure on the wavy sea
R olling left and right
E verything of gold was sparkling
A nd gold coins in a chest
S ail away with the treasure
U p the rigging
R ace to the island
E veryone start digging.

Broghan Collier (5)
Oakwood School, Oakwood

Cutlass

C urved metal
U p in the air
T he pirate holds it
L ong
A nd
S hiny
S word.

Archie Richardson (5)
Oakwood School, Oakwood

The Captain Hook Poem

H ard metal
O n his hand
O h no!
'**K** ill,' says Captain Hook.

Madeleine Boiardini (5)
Oakwood School, Oakwood

Captain Hook

C utlass sharp
A rm with a hook
P irate
T eeth that are rotton
A fierce face
I tchy boots
N ose wonky

H at black with a feather
O ld salty skin
O ut on his ship
K nife short and silver.

Poppy Chandler (6)
Oakwood School, Oakwood

The pirate

P irate ship
I n the storm
R ushing water
'A rgh!'
T he pirates on the ship say
E xciting sea air.

Emily Taylor (5)
Oakwood School, Oakwood

Black Beard

C utlass
A sword
P irate
T he pirate captain
A ye aye
I n the ship cabin
N asty pirate.

Oliver Curley (5)
Oakwood School, Oakwood

My First Acrostic 2011 - Sussex & Surrey

Treasure

T reasure is golden
R ow the boat to the island
E veryone on the boat
A coconut fell off
S hip ahoy
U p the rigging
R eady to fire the canons
E veryone back to bed.

Milly Betsworth (6)
Oakwood School, Oakwood

Pirate

P irate hiding treasure
I sail to an island
R igging lookout
A pirate ship is coming
T he pirates bury treasure
E veryone fires canons.

Francis Palmer (5)
Oakwood School, Oakwood

Pirate

P aper maps
I steer the wheel
R ight my hearties
A nchor dropped
T ea for pirates
E very pirate had eggs.

Benjamin Cotton (6)
Oakwood School, Oakwood

Ahoy There

A nchoring in the sea
H ello maties!
O y! Give me my treasure
Y ou can do some scrubbing

T ake the treasure
H ide under the deck
E very pirate gets gold
R un for it
E veryone's on board.

Isabel Harris (6)
Oakwood School, Oakwood

My First Acrostic 2011 – Sussex & Surrey

Treasure

T reasure is pirates' favourite
R igging blowing in the wind
E veryone scrubbing the boat
A pirate likes treasure
S hips on the sea
U p the rigging we go
R ide the waterfall
E very pirate finds treasure.

Charlotte Tennant (5)
Oakwood School, Oakwood

Ahoy There

A ll the pirates dancing
H ello I am Captain Skull
O ut of the ship now
Y ou are the best pirate

T he captain is scary
H e wants some treasure
E veryone go
R un for it
E veryone attack.

Jonathan Hoskins (5)
Oakwood School, Oakwood

Ahoy There

A ll aboard
H ello shipmates
O i you rascal come here!
Y ou can clean the decks

T hey are going to steal treasure
H ide it before they come
E veryone attack!
R un
E veryone got treasure.

Nicholas Sampson (5)
Oakwood School, Oakwood

Rafe

R unning
A nimals
F riendly
E gg.

Rafe Crane-Robinson (4)
Oakwood School, Oakwood

My First Acrostic 2011 - Sussex & Surrey

Cameron

C at
A nimals
M aking aeroplanes
E lephant
R unning races
O wls class
N ice school.

Cameron Sutherland (5)
Oakwood School, Oakwood

Henry

H appy
E xciting
N est
R unning
Y oyo.

Henry Harris (4)
Oakwood School, Oakwood

Amber

A nimals
M ousehole
B en in my class
E lephant
R afe is in my class.

Amber Street (4)
Oakwood School, Oakwood

Ruby

R ugby
U mbrellas
B utter
Y o-yos.

Ruby Chandler (4)
Oakwood School, Oakwood

Nieve

N ice
I ce cream
E xcited
V aluables
E aster.

Nieve Carson (5)
Oakwood School, Oakwood

My First Acrostic 2011 - Sussex & Surrey

Flight

F un
L onely
I nspiring
G reat
H appy
T hirsty children.

Ryan (6)
Springfield First School, Worthing

Flight

F lying hot air balloon.
L ovely balloon.
I nteresting view.
G iant sight.
H igh.
T hirsty.

Kai Nicholas (5)
Springfield First School, Worthing

Flight

F unny
L ucky
I nteresting
G ravity
H appy
T hirsty.

Ben Collins (6)
Springfield First School, Worthing

Flight

F unny
L ong
I nteresting
G ravity
H appy
T hirsty.

Kai (6)
Springfield First School, Worthing

Flight

F light is fantastic.
L ovely balloon flight.
I nteresting.
G reen trees.
H igh, high, high.
T hrough the clouds!

Lewis Cornford (6)
Springfield First School, Worthing

My First Acrostic 2011 - Sussex & Surrey

Flight

F at
L ucky
I nteresting
G ravity
H appy
T hirsty.

Ben Fisher (6)
Springfield First School, Worthing

Balloon

B alloon is fat
A sheep down low
L ucky
L ovely
O ver
O h no!
N oisy.

Jessi (6)
Springfield First School, Worthing

Balloon

B urner
A way
L onely
L ovely
O n a balloon
O ff the balloon
N oisy balloon.

Adara (6)
Springfield First School, Worthing

Balloon

B ad
A way
L onely
L ucky
O ver
O ver
N oisy.

Sumayyah Nawab (5)
Springfield First School, Worthing

Flight

F ly
L ight
I t does fly in the sky
G ravity
H appy
T he balloon goes up.

Ryan (6)
Springfield First School, Worthing

Flight

F lying
L ovely
I t is fun
G et in the basket
H appy
T hick clouds.

Kimberley Laird (6)
Springfield First School, Worthing

Flight

F antastic hot air balloon ride.
L onely rider.
I nteresting view.
G reat flight.
H ungry people.
T hirsy passengers.

Finlay (6)
Springfield First School, Worthing

Flight

F antastic Montgolfier brothers
L ovely hot air balloon
I nteresting view
G ravity
H ungry passengers
T errific balloon ride.

Finlay (6)
Springfield First School, Worthing

Flight

F ar away
L onely
I was happy that we survived
G reat flight
H ard landing
T he balloon was great.

Lara Mitchell (6)
Springfield First School, Worthing

My First Acrostic 2011 – Sussex & Surrey

Flight

F light
L ovely view
I like the view
G reat
H ungry
T he Montgolfier brothers.

Hannah Callahan (5)
Springfield First School, Worthing

Flight

F lights are really fun
L onely
I nteresting
G reat flight
H appy
T idy.

Luc Begej (5)
Springfield First School, Worthing

Balloon

F lying in the air
L ovely flight
I nteresting view
G reat day
H urrying
T rying hard to be brave.

Isabella Brady (6)
Springfield First School, Worthing

Flight

F unny balloon
L ovely flight
I love the Montgolfier balloon
G lad to be back
H appy to be back to my house
T ricky to get out of the basket.

Georgia Stowe (5)
Springfield First School, Worthing

Flight

F un
L ovely
I t is scary
G o up high
H igher
T ake time.

Joshua (6)
Springfield First School, Worthing

Flight

F lying
L onely
I nteresting
G ood
H appy
T hirsty.

Ethan Daniels (5)
Springfield First School, Worthing

My First Acrostic 2011 – Sussex & Surrey

Flight

F un
L ooking at the houses
I like the sheep
G ood ride
H elicopter
T ents down there.

Matilda (6)
Springfield First School, Worthing

George

G entle
E ats dark chocolate
O n the carpet
R eally clever
G ood
E ats ice cream.

George Hopper (5)
The Weald CE Primary School, Dorking

Mia

M akes crystals
I like playing with my friends
A lovely girl.

Mia Foskett (4)
The Weald CE Primary School, Dorking

Emily

E ats pasta
M agic
I ce cream eater
L ovely
Y our friend.

Emily Mae Fuller (5)
The Weald CE Primary School, Dorking

Charlie

C lever
H as Lego
A no slapping boy
R eally strong
L ovely
I am kind
E ats old McDonald's.

Charlie Harris (4)
The Weald CE Primary School, Dorking

My First Acrostic 2011 – Sussex & Surrey

Lola

L ovely
O n holiday
L ikes making cakes
A fantastic girl.

Lola Daniels (5)
The Weald CE Primary School, Dorking

Mia

M akes cakes
I like my cat
A ngel.

Mia Cooper (5)
The Weald CE Primary School, Dorking

Jake

J olly
A pple eater
K ind
E njoys building.

Jake Eastwood (5)
The Weald CE Primary School, Dorking

Lola

L ovley
O ff camping
L aughing
A nice girl.

Lola Watts (5)
The Weald CE Primary School, Dorking

Noah

N ice
O n top
A nimal lover
H appy.

Noah Jolly (4)
The Weald CE Primary School, Dorking

Hannah

H appy
A ngel
N ice
N ever naughty
A ctive
H oola hoop dancer.

Hannah Flashman (4)
The Weald CE Primary School, Dorking

My First Acrostic 2011 – Sussex & Surrey

Ethan

E ats pizza
T oy lover
H as a robot toy
A lovely boy
N ice.

Ethan Bond (4)
The Weald CE Primary School, Dorking

Lex

L oves Holly
E njoys playing
X cited.

Lex McIntosh (4)
The Weald CE Primary School, Dorking

Ryan

R eally likes building Lego spaceships
Y our friend
A kite maker
N ice.

Ryan Flashman (5)
The Weald CE Primary School, Dorking

Josh

J umps up and down
O n and off
S wimming is fun
H as a friend called Jay.

Joshua Thomas (4)
The Weald CE Primary School, Dorking

Oliver

O n a motorbike
L ovely
I am at school
V ery good friend
E ats pancakes
R uns fast.

Oliver Brien (4)
The Weald CE Primary School, Dorking

Winter

W et
I ndoors
N ot good weather
T rees have no leaves
E lf
R eady for Santa.

Miley James (6)
Westfield Primary School, Woking

My First Acrostic 2011 - Sussex & Surrey

Christmas

C andy
H olly
R eindeer
I ce
S leigh
T oys
M y presents
A ngels
S anta.

Benjamin Lewis
Westfield Primary School, Woking

Christmas

C andles burning
H ouses lit up
R eindeer come
I love Christmas
S anta comes
T oys
M y presents
A Christmas tree
S leigh.

Elise Cordery (6)
Westfield Primary School, Woking

Christmas

C hristmas tree
H ave presents
R eindeer
I cicle
S now
T ree
M agic
A Christmas treat
S anta comes.

Poppy-Bell Nash (5)
Westfield Primary School, Woking

Santa

S now
A ngel
N ew clothes
T urkey
A happy Christmas.

Nicole Crick-Marshall (6)
Westfield Primary School, Woking

My First Acrostic 2011 - Sussex & Surrey

Young Writers Information

We hope you have enjoyed reading this book - and that you will continue to enjoy it in the coming years.

If you like reading and writing poetry drop us a line, or give us a call, and we'll send you a free information pack.

Alternatively if you would like to order further copies of this book or any of our other titles, then please give us a call or log onto our website at www.youngwriters.co.uk.

Young Writers Information
Remus House
Coltsfoot Drive
Peterborough
PE2 9BF
(01733) 890066